SOME HOLY WEIGHT IN THE VILLAGE AIR

Also by Ira Joe Fisher

Remembering Rew (2004)

Some Holy Weight
in the
Village Air

POEMS

Ira Joe Fisher

ATHANATA ARTS, LTD.
GARDEN CITY, NEW YORK

ATHANATA ARTS, LTD.

Post Office Box 321
Garden City, New York 11530-0321
www.athanata.com

Copyright © 2006 by Ira Joe Fisher
All rights reserved
Printed in the United States of America
First Edition
NYQ Poetry Series, NO. I

ACKNOWLEDGMENTS

Grateful acknowledgment is made to the editors of the following journals
in which these poems first appeared: "Night," *Confrontation;* "February
Burial" & "Age," *Entelechy International;* "Only the Red-Winged Blackbird" &
"Aftermath," *The New York Quarterly;* "At the Height of Their Mischief,"
Poetry New York; "Winterlight," *Ridgefield Magazine*

Set in Berthold Baskerville Book
Designed by Peter Arcese

ISBN–10: 0-9727993-2-X
ISBN–13: 978-0-9727993-2-4

… for Dear and Gus
and the little valley where they lived …

Contents

Vantage

Snow Walk	12
Arrival	15
A Storm and an Old Coupe	16
Between the Night and the Day	19
Banker's Progress	20
A Moment	22
Broken Again	23
At the Height of Their Mischief	24
The Bird Bath	25
Inevitable	26
All That's Left	27
The Brevity of Misappropriation	30
On Second Thought	31
And Out in the Kitchen	32
Mystery	33
The Maple and the Pine	34
The Man Who Lived at the Dump	35
What I Had Forgot	39
The Dairyman's Wife	40
Staying Put	44
The Cattaraugus Wind	45

Together	48
Trees and the Wind	49
Only to the Sun	51
Some Holy Weight in the Village Air	52
Sculpting	56
Only the Red-Winged Blackbird	58
Clouds, Houses, Hills	60
Darkest	61
February Burial	64
Remembering Rew	65
Glance	69
Forget It	70
Winterlight	73
Waiting	74
Fall Leaves Fall	76
Something I Could Not Tell You	77
What is Seen	78
Someone Else's Supper	79
Aftermath	81
Age	82
Night	83
There Comes Each Year One Fall Day	84

SOME HOLY WEIGHT IN THE VILLAGE AIR

Vantage

Sometimes the heightened, nightened hills
Blink the blinks of fireflies.
Hear the wind sigh in the trees
At the doings in the village down below?

Snow Walk

From the crusted snow the boy looks back,
Down hill to the clump of houses he
And his brother left a half-hour ago.
The light from the front room lamp
Of their house seeps on the snow.
The boy's clothes are lumpy and warm.
The buckles on his arctics clink
As he stomps to keep up with the brother
Who is ten years older and never smiles.
Even when the wind cackles and sparkles
In the loose snow over the crust.
With a sigh his brother says, *It is midnight.*
The boy only knows him to march
Into the woods and hunt, firing
A deep, in-the-trees crack dropping
A squirrel, a deer, a woodchuck to death
On the side of the hill. His brother seems
To need to hunt. But tonight,
They're off on a walk, telling no one.
They're off on a walk and the brother brings
The boy instead of his gun. And he only speaks
To teach or scold: *Those are deer tracks.*
Cover your ears.
Woodchucks have two holes to their homes.
Keep up.

This ... is wintergreen.
Red berries in brittle December.
The brother offers one from his
Un-gloved palm. It tastes clean and soft
To the boy, a berry that waits for winter,
Grows fat on snow. He chews
And watches his brother chew: bony cheeks
Catch moonlight; then lose it
In the creases around his mouth.
The brother spits and frowns
And barks, *We must go.* Birch branches
Tune the wind to a minor key.
The snow in the woods, on the meadow
Is drifted so packed and hard
They walk on it. In that glow between earth
And the moon, the snow won't break.
A leaf shudders on a sugar maple.
The boy smells the wet wool
Over his nose and mouth. He still tastes
Wintergreen. They crunch out
Of the trees; the brother hisses, *Stop.*
And the boy stops. Everything.
Walking and breathing and hearing
The leaves. *Listen.* The brother glares
Off and away, up hill. The boy listens.

A creek gurgles in a black
cavern beneath the snow. From
Crystal-edged holes, vapor rises and catches
The moon and makes of it glittering things.
The boy looks up at his brother, who looks off
To the woods. The boy wonders if
His brother sees a deer or a fox.
And why the night can not make him happy.

Arrival

With the window breeze
a glass of water cools the morning.

The leaves in the trees
Speak of a storm forming.

A grumbling in the air
(Slanting rain; likely lightning,

A winded, wooshed hellion dare)
Might mean rage, just might bring
An old-photo dark to this Annville day.

A Storm and an Old Coupe

The night glows gold
along the cloud's torn edges.
A stilled electric smell pries
from my mind an old scene.

I am a boy in a summer. I hunch
on the fuzzy shelf under the rear window
of an old coupe belonging to a man name of Newton.
Quiet lightning winks in the quiet night
saving thunder for that sweet moment
of wind raging with rain. Night glowers
through the window of the auto
swaying on the road through the hills.
The man name of Newton drives.
My mother rides passenger.
They ignore the charred, conspiring sky
and gossip about the old grocery
where they work: the butcher Ernie
smiling from the middle of his blue-veined face;
old, odd Tom, the owner,
grinding peanuts and eating the butter
to hide the sting in his breath;
and Luella punching the cash register
with her one good hand, the other chewed down
to a finger and a thumb, during the war,

by a canning machine,
in a factory now five years closed.
The dashboard dusts a feeble amber
light on them and their talk of waiting
on villagers and farmers
who wear stained clothes,
buy margerine, call it oleo,
and tuck their beer
behind the sack of potatoes.
I bump small behind my mother
and the man name of Newton,
a hiding spy on the talk
of two who are years beyond
wonder at a summer storm.
I marvel at the night, I count its thuds,
I flatten my palm
on the window studding with rain.
The storm commits, now, to storming.
Lightning paints on the back of my mind.
I turn to the front
from my window-shelf perch
and insane rain yellows in the headlights.
Two winds wrestle for the coupe:
the wind it wakes in speeding;
the wind the storm blows across its path.

I sigh a sigh that asks
how this storm could not pull their minds
away from a sagging store
whose floor creaks beneath
scarred linoleum. I curl and shiver
and listen on the hard, scratching
shelf behind my mother and a man
name of Newton, whose talk
of the people falls below
the ranting, raging storm
snarling and spitting and demanding,
like a beheading king, to be noticed
by two peasants and a servant boy,
as it blusters and swears
outside the rear window of an old coupe.

Now I sit, gray as the tree-poked sky
no nearer knowing, sniffng the air,
peering neck-bent over the top of the house.
Hoping this night might rain.

Between the Night and the Day

A new cloud, its underside sunning
in stumbling dawn, hangs

above the road. Willows
and the hay-hill lift

to greet the morning god-glow.
Night and day weaving

in this coming-and-leaving,
this powdered passing

of atoms, this two source stream
giddy and back from hidden places,

night and day sift through
the same blended, loomed light;

night forsaking the valley,
as day climbs the eastern sky.

Banker's Progress

Walls and beams and rafters
are dying a wooden death
under tar-paper bricks stained
and grainy. The leaning grocery sinks
under oaks and elms like a box
emptied of something forgot.
Through the rippled window,
from a place yellow and smokey,
a flourescent light recalls
a time when Ruben, in his apron,
sliced meat and sold beer to railroad gangs
in west end Annville. I picked up
the papers for my route from stacks
on the store porch. Trudy worked
the register up front. And grew old
with Ruben. They sold each day
until dark, even in summer, and walked
home apart, I watched them, to different
houses, different spouses. I drank
a birch beer; then, pedaled my bike away
to peddle my papers. The store grayed
like the iron sky over the Allegheny.
Ruben's face grew doughey; he smiled
at the jokes of the railroad men.
He looked away from the women,

including Trudy, whose teeth went
with the years. She blamed the drop
in business on Route Seventeen
re-cutting beyond town; that and a market
at the mall. Ruben blamed no one.
He just looked out the rippled window.
At the leaves? At the leaves struggling
from buds; lighting with summer and mercury
vapor; drooping into autumn? Did he just look
out that rippled window at the blur
over all he saw?

Snow plugged the walk and drifted
on the porch. A chain hung from the door
latch. With my coat-collar up over my ears
I stood and looked at that chain.
I heard sleet and snow in the wind
Needling the glass, the front, the shingles.
I touched the mail slot, thinking to melt
the rust and furry ice with my fingertips.
And, under oaks and elms and litter
growing over left-alone tracks,
I shivered—with dread or some sweet
knowing?—at ghosts who rose
in the emptied store.

A Moment

A jet's frosty tail scores
the high
blue sky.
Winds rake
gaps across it.
Then, in the sparking
sun, the straight
thin thread
trembles,
dis-
sem
bles.
The cold drone
of the engine's
held note
and the speck
of the jet
sound
a warning
of war.

Broken Again

Long ago snow whistled down from heaven
or a cloud alighting in sweeps and drifts.
At night the arctic wind tuned the trees,

and cut on the roof into a thousand
curling winds that polished the yard to glass.
I rode the unclouded morning on a sled

and laughed 'til I thought the day would crack.
Age wrested the sled and hung it in the cellar
where it dried and splintered and grayed.

I was ordered into uniform. And heard
cursed words of war. Snow grayed
in the shadow of a flag. Snow grayed

and lay smooth. War spills
on snow. Flashes, cries, rumbles, blood.
But, again, last night winter whistled down

from heaven or a cloud, sweeping
and drifting and calling my children.
I thought their thoughts behind their eyes

as I watched through the window. The rubble
sparkled in their play in heaped, sled-sliced ridges.
The snow was broken again.

At the Height of the Their Mischief

Starlings mobbed the sky
and looked like laughter.
They flew too fast to follow;
it was good to watch from below
as they burst above the day.
Their tumbling feathers
against the clouds
shook some worried thing
out of the moment.
And the sun, behind the hill,
sent word it saw
what the starlings were up to:
it lighted them yellow-orange
in one quick, burnished turn.
At the height of their mischief
these starlings delayed winter
by playing in the very air
that, in the cold, always
fills with dread.

The Bird Bath

The sky brushes jagged
gray over the blue. I scuff
down an alley behind houses
where buds haven't stirred
enough to wake the elms.

Robins pipe a watery chortle.
Still too much winter in the world.
But robins fly to mind when I spot
an old stone bird bath
behind an old stone house.

A brambled lawn
the color of smoke at the dump,
dotted with rocks
and trellesses
and set-aside hopes.

Are birds leery of some seering
power in the bath? If they perch
upon it, will they turn to stone
on a lawn as good as a grave?

Inevitable

The confused bramble woods,
(maples, oaks, beeches,
birches and dogwood) are barred
from the sloping meadow
by a straight break of pines.
What must the hawk have thought
when she lifted to look?
And sweet to the ear of the deer
when the wind whispered
at sunset. But, the hay rake is rusted.
It sinks into the brown bent grass
that failed to make one more hay.
The farmer hobbled off the field
to the leaning porch where he
pulled off his rubber boots
marbled with mud and dung.
The boots cooled and dried
his sweat from the second cutting
into the last cutting.

All That's Left

The smoke from the chimney draws
a line from the house to heaven,
keeping the two from getting any closer
or any farther apart.
The barn shows day between
the wallboards, but the sun dies
in the rust of the cows' water bowls.
The rats and cats are gone,
the hay bales settle and sag.
Dung no longer stings the air.
The chaff is dropped and settled.
Out in the yard the clothesline poles lean
to the end of their rope;
the pin bag droops. The flagstone path
from the barn to the house is tufted
with grass worn out from growing.
The fence of posts and wire
lets down its guard. The fence of stones,
thrown at the meadow from space,
or climbing from frosted, deep earth,
has tumbled and widened
from wind and snow and snakes.
But for a here-and-there pebble,
the drive is down to dust.
And in the house,

where overalls hang on a hook;
where the coffee has cooled;
and the empty dog dish has been bumped
under the stove, the clock's click has stopped.
In the parlor, in a fuzzy wingback with doilies,
a woman sits. And all that moves
in that dusk-dimmed room
where a bookcase and pictures
of aunts bleed into the wall,
are the woman's eyes
behind wire-rim glasses.
Her eyes and the tremble of her chin
are all that moves.
We never know
a slowing down
is really
the work
of stopping.
The mud-flecked boots will be pulled off
And dropped on the porch forever.
The pitchfork stabs
the last hay
of the last, long day.
Dishes are washed,
mugs are hung,

and the door on the cupboard is shut.
The not-believed end comes.
And in this house on this farm
by a field in brown November,
all that moves
are the eyes and chin
of a woman in the parlor.
And the chimney smoke rises
toward heaven and thins
and bends
and breaks.

The Brevity of Misappropriation

This low, gray day carries an illusion.
The rain first roars, then after roaring
Rises fog-weary from its intrusion,
Returning to mother sky from scouring
The clover-cluttered ground, gray and fog-bound.
Above tufted shrubs and Queen Anne's lace
There floats a haze, like a hovering frown.
The rain retreats to quench with gathering grace
A far fern field lumped with thirsty flowers;
A willow and a maple and a beech.
To seep, to drip in dark glowered bowers.
Such rain, ages-wise, has such things to teach.
Duty-sworn to hit the hay; it can't stay.
Leave the cloud, return to cloud. It's rain's way.

On Second Thought

After the sere time
when night was only dimmed day
and leaves were old in August
rain fell.
It looked at first like other things:
tailor's thread on a new-sewn suit;
fireflies jetting
to death. It looked
at first in the headlights
like scribbles from a sparkler
on a Fourth of July forty years ago.
And the moment it hit
the grass and gravel it turned
and rose in steam,
a slower rain returning
to the mother cloud, going back
a ghost of obedience,
shamed and gray and floating
as if falling were some mistake.

And Out in the Kitchen

The glass table top
in the restaurant
chills my arms.
Coffee, the color
of spring snow,
droops in lines
down the side of the cup
like worn sorrow.
And out in the kitchen
behind the groaning doors
a dish, a cup, a bowl—
something—breaks.
Laughing
and applause.
In the first note
of ruin do those revelers
feel guilt for what
they've dropped? An ancient,
childish regret at this
broken moment?
Do sorry thoughts search
the universe for the old,
offended moulder of the clay?

Mystery

Across the counter and muffin crumbs,
through coffee steam,
under a crackling neon cigarette,
the waitress with brown hair squeezes
the dimpled arm
of the waitress who is blonde.
Peering over the top of her glasses,
dipping her chin to her neck,
she whispers through her lipstick:
Don't push the minestrone.
Wrinkles spread north
from her now-clenched mouth.
That wave sends her eyebrows climbing.
The blonde nods
as if she'd just confirmed
a raw rumor about the wife
of that fellow in the bow tie
over at the post office.
She clumps away,
cradling four plates of burgers.
I look down into my soup.
Something's up with the minestrone.

The Maple and the Pine

How heavened is this moment: a tall, black pine,
washed by the shadow of a cloud, is caught
grieving in front of a flaring round maple
on fire from the fall, on fire from the sun.
The maple's giving-up leaves are leaving;
impudently exploding around and through
the drooping gloom of the pine.

The Man Who Lived at the Dump

Skinny, beaky, with a pipe in his mouth
Instead of teeth; laughing, breathing through his nose
Lucius sorted his days at the dump. He
Had a nice house, I heard, a nice house
(Yellow clapboard and green shutters) over
On Fair Oak Street, but he lived at the dump.
Sifting through the garbage. I saw him:
Gray coveralls every day. Coveralls
And a stained old Dodger cap. His shoes had been
Shiny, once, but now they were scraped and dusty.
Some nights, they tell, he'd sleep in his dented
Buick; an old wreck the color of clouds
Before a storm. Folks said he had a nice
Place over on Fair Oak, but he lived
Among the things the village threw away:
Mustard jars, leaking batteries, a flattened
Catcher's mitt, fuzzy gray clothesline with pins
Still here and there, baskets trailing dry flowers
Or pieces of cheese, green beer bottles,
Brown beer bottles and wrinkled pots and pans.
He sorted and he sifted and some of it
He saved; saved in a shack behind a padlocked
Door. Lucius'd open it up with a key
At the end of a gray string from somewhere
In his coveralls. Why'd he lock such things

Away? Every day he'd scuff into that shack
With razor strops, smelly quilts, davenport springs,
One of those radios with the yellow dial.
Lucius carried things into that shack
And he never carried any thing out. Dog collars,
Shirt collars, hub caps and buckets.
He carried every thing in and he never carried
Any thing out. And the shack never changed;
It stayed small and weathered and gray.
It could've stood some paint, but never got any
And Lucius just kept adding to its store.
And folks'd talk. How'd it hold his every
Thing? I always wondered if it was like the piling
Of the years. Always room to go in with all
The other years. Room for breath and light.
I have to say I wondered if Lucius' shack
Was like the place that keeps the years. Could he
Put any thing in any amount into it?
Was that something Lucius could do?
Like light his pipe or trip on a soup can
Or cut his shoes or haul out a key
At the end of a string? I mean the *outside*
Of the shack never changed, it just stayed withered
And gray and splintery, but inside
Was there something … some thing

Pure and clean and polishing? In the middle
Of this dump, where rats played with disease like a toy,
Was there a place—this shack—purged of dirt
And evil? Did Lucius save the junk he saved
So he could save himself? Save himself and
Take himself into a shack in the middle
Of a dump when his day to die came
And he figured he'd be thrown away?
All I know is one day, years after,
I came across a clipping that the dump
In the town exploded. Yes. Exploded.
Folks had feared there must've been dynamite
Stored somewhere under it all. And lightning
Or hellions or maybe, I thought, maybe
An old man in coveralls pulled out his key
One last time, stooped through the door and
Scuffed to some boxes he had saved
(Boxes of long red sticks that he'd been piling
Stick by stick right by the pile of years)
Maybe Lucius found those boxes
Hidden under an ironing board, Collier's
Magazines and boots with holes in their soles.
What if Lucius clumped over to an oak night stand
Balancing a bad leg on a box of blue-tip matches
And struck a bargain with himself in a dark,

cold hole deeper than where he hid his keys,
And he kept a vow, said a word,
And struck a match. Maybe he struck
A match and lit up that shack and
... and took it all with him.

What I Had Forgot

Winter came yesterday and knocked the leaves
off October. All that's left are sticks.
It was a rain and not snow but more click
in its fall than sizzle. This morning
on my walk I watch the hardiest leaves yield
and sink stem-ahead down, soft in a circle,
to the grass and road. I look at these leaves
in their grave attitude and I see
what I had forgot: how the rain rests
on them; round drops, intact, complete; so perfect
I want to put them in a box to hide
up in my room. The rain on the leaves,
down on the grass and road, takes the morning
and shapes light into something small and shining.

The Dairyman's Wife

Age took the world, a piece at a time,
from Edith. When she sat
with her daughter's children
and talked the talk of the old,
it was of her girlhood. How she
walked the summer barefoot, saving
her shoes for school in the fall.
She told of launching a baby brother
in a rickety wagon from the top
of the farm's high lawn. It rattled
to a bump against a rock
at the edge of the crayfish creek,
one wheel spinning; the other smashed,
her brother crying and fine.
The wagon and the rock and her tales
of last century are blurred
and buried; grown over with trees.
Edith's farmer-husband Cullen died.
They loved when they were young.
They courted and married
and drove in a buggy
to his farm. Their life was fields,
a gnarled orchard,
the barn, the hay and cows
and a clapboard house

with a bed upstairs, a tin tub
in the kitchen for bathing
and in the parlor a bible
they only opened to inscribe a death.
Their life was work and sweat.
No cooling until groaning winter
breathed ice on the pond.
Edith never questioned any of it,
even the day Cullen died
and left her with her widowhood.
She sold what had been their life
for a square of land
below a hill, beside a creek,
along a road of few autos.
And there she lived, rising before dawn,
like a dairyman's wife,
to sit by the front room window. She sat
and sorted scraps for rugs and quilts.
Her flowered dress and apron lace;
Edith sewed them both.
I'll never wear a boughten thing.
Her meals were grown and found:
peas and potatoes with chives
that sprouted like soft, green hair
by the trampled path to the mailbox.

In the garden she picked squash
and spinach and beans.
But she never saw age take the world,
a piece at a time, leaving
dwindled thoughts.
Thunder scared her:
Lightning will hit the barn.
The rain might soak the new-cut hay—
it musn't go in the barn wet.
Wind might knock down the August corn.
Now, in her mateless dark,
Edith would say to her grandchildren:
Birds on the electric line: rain's a comin'.
I feel a dread, go turn a stone down in the dust.
The crick is runnin' smooth,
winter'll spend a month under zero.
And as the world beyond her window
dimmed, God peopled her view.
One morning when she went
to get a pan for eggs,
snakes—it looked like a hundred of them—
rippled through the kitchen drawer.
She took it as a sign from God
to get out of the house.
So, she did.

She died.
After she was buried
with the dirt on the mound
still brown,
an auto screamed down
the road,
veered off
and into Edith's place
exploding the summer dark;
settling splinters over the lawn.

Staying Put

The snow was wisped upon the hill
(Its cloud had but a bit to spill).

It looked to me from down below
More *grass* was on the hill than snow,

As it should be in later spring.
But now the hill was wintering

And should, in sun, be bluish white
And give the hill a ghosted sight.

My eyes discerned a wobbly path
Like a dead creek's dried aftermath,

Its currents gone, its course forgot
(From sun too near and far too hot).

The path was white upon the hill
(The cloud gave just the *path* its fill).

Or it looked to me to be so
And I simply stayed down below.

The Cattaraugus Wind

Evening folds over the kitchen.
He looks at his schoolbooks stacked
on the table and draws lines
in the toast crumbs still there
from breakfast. The beagle flattens
into furry sleep beside
the chuffing refrigerator.
From the center of the faded, sagging ceiling
the fluorescent light paints the kitchen
into the window's night mirror.
The boy blows air from his lips up
across his face. He hears autos whooshing
by on the road. He is thinking
of doing something that would make
his father angrier. He is thinking
of leaving. A boy can catch a car with his thumb
and a ride away from an aiming
finger; a cursing word. He believes
any next town can blossom
a life in the *front* of the mind.
He thinks of spitting on that cramped brick
house, where roses climb a trellis
and two maples hold a hammock.

In darkness woven of night
and dread, he thinks of thumbing
a ride on the Cattaraugus wind.

When he was small he dreamed
a dream so etched with grass
and sun that he remembered
it for years as real: his brother scooped
him up into his arms, grabbed the tail
of a kite that lifted them
a hundred feet above the field.
He looked down, down on the waving
grass, Guernsey cows
and a border collie, black and white
and frantic at boys in the sky.
He thinks of that kite flight every day,
but talks of it no more
down the disbelieving years. Couldn't
that wind have woven through the woods,
down the hills around the brick house
and spirited him away from rage
smelling of port wine? Couldn't
he have blown away to a town of small houses,
neighbors playing catch,
sharing their porch
and waving from a chair on a cool, long lawn?

But such thoughts are just thoughts,
sketched in toast crumbs. The boy sighs,

smooths the rolled-up cuffs on his shirt
and pushes the thought back down deep
on top of his courage and he just sits.
Just sits and thinks that bumming
a ride carries a made-up story.
It means sitting beside the driver
and pretending to look straight
through the windshield. Pretending
to look straight through the windshield
at something worth seeing ahead.

Together

The time is well-yeared into October.
From a shuddering train I catch
A tree. Its leaves and sketching
Twigs suggest *one* tree;
But, as my glance slips
From high down to the bulging ground,
I see two trunks;
I see two trees.
Each so like the other
And close, tangling their branches.
Then, I see the leaves
On the southside tree
Blasted yellow dipped in red.
The tree on the north still hangs
A summer green. Cold sneaked
From a surprise direction
And spun one with fall.
The other tree offers limbs still full
With sap. The train clacks on
Not slowed at all
By two trees I've seen
and recall down the track.

Trees and the Wind

Curious trees and the wind always take time
to talk, to gossip. A breezy catching-up.
In winter harsh, brittle, sparkled,
the wind complains to creaking trees
to let the moon down.

Then, the white roots and dirt crumbs
and filling-in shadows of spring: softly
speaking of yellow-green sprigs and airy,
powered pieces making sneezes.
Their talk is haughty and beyond me.

Is there a ranting about holding the earth
and stroking it? And where was that smell hiding?
Do curious trees and the wind know ghosts?
Does the birch tell the poplar a story
of beef and beets and eyes falling shame?

Perhaps the wind skitters in the pines so aging maples
will know where the waked leaves rest and how the pods
fair? Are there tales of orcharded apples
and pulpy pears who don't hear well anymore
(their work stolen as if they were serfs)?

I listen, but bundled and muffled and wrapped away
from the cleared air, I don't understand.
I am low and lost. I fail to learn why chestnuts fall
and firs bow. And how all keep secret
the secrets of trees and the wind.

Only to the Sun

I sit looking out at Annville
through a rippled window
that takes autumn and waves it,
the colors of the leaves like a flag
flapping allegiance to the sun.

Some Holy Weight in the Village Air

In the bars, in the two hotels, sunlight from over
the tops of the hills finds the bottles in the mirror.
In each bar an unshaved man in gray pants
and gray shirt hushes the morning with a broom.
This invading sun reddens each man's arms
and eyes or so he thinks with an aching head.
He sweeps the dust up into the slanting sun.
And sweeps a tongue over his gums.
The town of two hotels fills
the little valley. The hills look away
and give their lean and leanness to farms;
farms that grow wheat and rocks,
corn and cattle and hay. And the farms
sink poorer and deeper into exhausted hills.
Mornings, as they milk
the cows, farmers feel that their drink-drummed
heads are squeezed in a like way. Farm
and town bedrooms sour, in the rising light,
from the drunken night before. Lies pile on lies;
the worst (a nip every day with the fellows,
just being a pal) are those the self says to the self.
To town truck the farmers in a procession
of denim and wool. They bear cows' milk,
to pay for grain
to give the cows

to make the milk
to pay for grain.
And in the two hotels they buy their beer.
The larger is the Rock City which honors
a nearby forest of glacial stones the mists
left when the mists melted. This hotel offers
a long, curving bar, mugs, ash trays, ring stains,
and a jar of pickled eggs. A side room
sports a pool table and a game of cards
called "Fish," with a laugh, when the deputy
comes by on rounds. In fall deer hang
from the porch while their killers sway
at the bar inside boasting tales
of bloody snow. The second hotel is smaller;
its bar three-sided and short.
Sawdust on the floor, the taproom always dark;
its light swallowed as if it were lager.
This is the Milks Hotel,
named for the family who built it.
There's a front alcove just wide enough
for a shuffle board, narrow enough
for spider webs on the window panes.
The Milks is the fathers' hotel: a shot,
a draught, a tumbler of cheap wine.
Some of the men are just elbows and knees,

propped on the stools; cigarette smoke rippling
gray in the air like drowning-water.
Some are bellies falling over scarred belts.
Thick spectacles bulge half-closed eyes above
radish noses. The Milks Hotel settles
with the dust that settles with the years under
old maples who talk, when the wind blows,
about the liquid life beneath them.
The Milks Hotel settles with the dust
just down the street from the Methodist Church,
whose bells, at noon and night and funerals,
cause the drinking fathers to start
and snap their eyes like rubber bands in the hope
God isn't calling. The telephone rings
up a similar hope about wives at home
wiping toast crumbs off their kitchen tables.
Boys fish in Brick Pond, fed by Cattaraugus
Creek; and kill squirrels with twenty-twos, making
their fathers proud. Girls dance with each other
and know every word of every song.
Their mothers cook and clean and sigh.
Some holy weight in the village air
hangs in the ring of time, turning night into
morning, pulling at liquid in a lover's
eyes, quickening her breathing and stirring her.

It can fill a man's head with hate
and make him kill. In the air and dust that cling
to the leaves swirl an old woman's past,
the thundered pride of an old man's mistakes.
A father heavy-foots to a dirty job.
A mother slippers to the sink. Boys up and out,
prowl for baseball or a cat in the creek.
A too-old woman with home-permanent hair
scuffs her way to clean a rich woman's house.
Girls live in missed moonlight, learn to sew.
And the air yellows, turns brittle
and smells of a room we don't enter anymore.

Sculpting

This day breaks the work
of the clouds coloring the sky.

Little rags of blue scrape the grey,
their edges combed vapor.

Sudden sunlight, trembling
the poplar leaves, shudders

shade on the winded grass.
Then, comes a cooling.

All this colors the air yellow,
the unpeopled plot strange

beneath the clouds.
The tree rises to reach

a fitful rain
that begins low, rises

to see what it can see
and falls again to the tree.

Day, poplar, and grass
burst blossoming

to shape this moment
with air and lighted green.

Only the Red-Winged Blackbird

The song burbles curving
Into a room where
I'm housed against the heat.
It flutes like a stream through the screen
On the metal-scented wind;
And carries me along a long ago:
Up on a mossy hill where I sat
Counting the steeples and smokestacks
Of Annville below.
I wondered which caused
Clouds and what to make
Of the sleek slip of hours.
A red-winged blackbird's song
Trilled from a clover field
Where an old man in denim
Stooped and tried to teach me
How to swing a scythe;
Where a border collie
And a beagle, wearied
By faster rabbits, slept in the dust.
I see a warping wood farm house
And a red tractor with cobwebs whiffling
In its wheels. The birdsong carries
The buzz of bothering flies
And Holstein cows flicking their tails.

Cows who always knew when to moo
And when to slog home to the barn.
Oh, there were other birds:
Nervous swallows sewing
Rafters and roofs;
Jays in bully-blue screeching
And taunting; starlings in praise
Of reeds and the creek; robins peeping
Night into day; and wrens dressed
Like squat brown friars caring
Neither to spin nor reap.
But only the red-winged blackbird
Ripples a watery song
From summers gone to ghosts.
Only the red-winged blackbird
Can lump a song with the ripples
Of times I let leave, to haunt me
In the shadow of my room.

Clouds, Houses, Hills

Snow and the ragged blue above it
make the day glassy cold.
Cinder dust thrown, god-fearing,
at the last storm seeps
to the side of the street.
Two gulls hold a roof-peak
and cough in the January wind,
glazing from the north.
Trees only sense
the sun, reach for it,
and scratch scars
into clouds, houses, hills
and the heart of anyone
looking in this day
for some good.

Darkest

There needs to come a quieting.
Winds must slow, must stop,
Must settle like a pollen of ghosts
Upon Annville
Where no building climbs
Higher than five stories.
Shingles weary of catching
Moonlight above the thuds and
Creaking floors in rented rooms
Over the Milks hotel bar.
Neon should not crackle all night,
There needs to come a quieting.
The gray rag that wipes
The bar droops and dries
On a nail beneath washed glasses,
Emptied to the dark. Out on Erie street
A last car flutters a last maple seed.
Above the gutter the sidewalk
Is black-streaked from bicycle tires
Flapping poker cards in their spokes
To rattle like something big.
After boys and noise and radio songs
Sung by girls dying to smile
There needs to come a quieting.
Between last-calls for draughts

And the clank of the milk-man
The village settles in heavy lead dark.
Within a ring of elms the school sinks
Like chalk dust into night. In the church
Across Thompson Avenue
The smell of withered hymnals hangs
In the air like an organ note
Too weak to leave,
Too light to be heard.
And the bible on the pulpit
Bleeds black into the night;
Bleeds black and is gone.
To the frame-house whose shutters,
Their green paint stuck, won't shut,
There needs to come a quieting.
On the clover lawn the bees are gone
And the bicycle lies on its side
Licked by the night with dew.
In the house, through the parlor,
Where a grandmother and her never-wed
Daughter sew years and squares
Into quilts, the light under the stairs
Is out. Dreams stir the sleeping boy.
His bed wrinkles from his troubling,
Dreams of heavy legs

Too slow to reach the receding door;
Panicked by the scent of wine
Leering behind, from a shadow
That grows until he wakes
To the lost sights of night.
There needs to come a quieting.
The dim clock glows
With other stopped hands,
Frozen fingers, eyes wide
And worrying the dark
As if it were a stone
Thrown in anger.
There the boy lies listening
For the floor to groan
Or the door to whine
On its hinges. Even in blank silence
With the dream powdering away,
Not opening, not happening,
Even then, his sleep is done.
He knows the clock glow
Will devil into day.
He listens between heart beats;
He listens, too paralyzed to pray.
There needs to come a quieting.

February Burial

Blowing snow
blurs his eyes
as he scuffs down
the slope from her grave.
Wind throws
the snow up
into the snow.
The sky is all cloud,
except where the sun
bores a hole
just over the hill.

Remembering Rew

The wind is no friend tonight,
razzing through the trees,
scraping Fawn's neck and cheek;
there's no looking in its eye.
Snow swirls around her feet.
Biting ice ruffles her hair.
Her shoulders reach to cover
her uncovered ears.
Her legs, in a skirt, tremble,
trying to warm in air
that slips rudely through.
And this blue numbing squeezes a tear.
How many winters will an old woman
see? Shaking on that town corner
in a worn-away coat and fuzz-ball scarf,
Fawn looks up Stoll street,
into the wind, at the dry snow wisping
on the sidewalk. Her stockings
wrinkle above her boots
beneath her flapping hem.
Her gray hair flutters and
snow blurs the blocks
of Annville tilting Fawn's mind
into 1933, when she and Grant
lived on an oil lease above Rew.
It was there that caused her,

in the piling years, to say that Pennsylvania
pulled winter down to a new low.
Brittle cold, drifting snow, Grant
gone six days from dark to dark caring
for the oil pumps; heavy-footing
home for supper and sleep, smelling
of tobacco and grease. All Fawn had
was a radio. A radio crackling
stories out of Bradford. And sometimes
a song in the falling winter night. A song
recalling a barn dance and waltzing
with Grant when love seemed
a good idea. As the song filled
the kitchen, Fawn'd stand at the sink
as lights from the house glowed
out on the smooth, amber snow;
the light fell, widened
and faded in a way Fawn knew well.
The sparkle of the lights
Or leaving day or the moon
through the trees, through
the misted snow seemed to say
some thing Fawn could not hear.
Did the sparkles ask her to come?
to dance? to twirl and whirl

in the swirling wind? Did the sparkles
ask her to step out into the
widened light before it faded,
before it broke, before the song
settled like dust at dawn
on a ballroom floor?
She'd look from the radio
to the reddening sky over
snow-plugged Pennsylvania smelling
of woodsmoke and soap.
A knock one noon on the peeling-
paint door brought a young man
in gray clothes, shivering and sorry,
to take the radio away. Too many
months without a payment
silenced the radio and turned the wind
to the only music Fawn heard.
Those years scrape these years.
Salted snowbanks lay in lines
along Goldfinch Lane and Stoll Street.
Fawn's marbled eyes flutter
and struggle and fail.
Now, she knows only this:
her happiness took ill and died
in a house on a hill above Rew.

And these are just thoughts
brought from even further away.
And each time she folded them,
she lifted them to a shelf growing
too high to reach. The only thoughts
it's easy to reach, now, are broken
heaps of dim winter and
the wind is no friend tonight.

Glance

My headlights bathe a vine
as I scratch around a dusty corner.
Autumn has drained
the leaves yellow.
In this too-quick turn
in the too-quick night
the vine hangs like the tentacle
of a dryly dying octopus
thirty sad miles from the sea.

Forget It

Who cares if Uncle Louie was tight with his
money? Or if Doodles Hill was in a family way

on her wedding day? Imagine a body interested in
Teddy telling how he once shook Edison's hand.

There's a photo somewhere, somebody says,
of a fellow named Carney working in the thirties

on a beam they were raising on the Chrysler
Building. And how about Lottie?

After Herm her dad, and Dan her hubby died,
she kept the farm for twenty-two years

and never paid a bill. She was a heroine
to everyone in the county. Except the lawyers.

I hear she'd hide behind the manure pile
whenever the sheriff came to foreclose.

He never stayed or looked for long. (Well,
crimefighting works up a thirst.)

You demand I tell about Peachy—
a barber named "Peachy." His fingers

twitched from all those years snipping.
And he breathed so many clippings

there was more hair in his lungs
than on his head. Bert, at the bar,

suggested that Peachy inhale a comb.
In case he ever needed an autopsy.

And wouldn't you like to learn about
Addie Pettle Carmichael who lost a foot

in a bootlegging accident on the Peace Bridge
between Canada and Buffalo?

Oh, the stories, you cry! Oh, the tales!
The lives, you pipe, have got to be remembered!

It's a history that has to be passed down.
Oh, really, I think. Oh ... really.

Tell about these hellions and robbers and scamps?
They lied. They fought. They voted Republican.

And now the lot is dead, damned and dumped
in the grave. Tell their stories? Please.

Winterlight

Just the right gray
The clouds and trees and day.
The snow is resting
After a calm sifting,
After raging in furies
All night.
Now the twigs
Are lined white
And lay the little light
Ten in the morning allows
Across woods
Across lawns
Lumped and humped and soft
With just the right gray
Of clouds and trees and day.

Waiting

A red toolbox sits on the stone
that served as a step for seventy years
to the porch of the house
by the train station.
The house is beginning to bend
from the weight of the moss
on its roof.
I dance from foot to foot,
waiting for the train
and watch my breath
rag into the blue air.
For seventy years
the house has heard
the ping-song in the tracks
of the coming train.
The early orange of winter evening
glows through the upstairs window.
The toolbox and a coil of cord
the color of the sky
wait on that cold, stone step
below the porch that bows.
Did cigar ashes and spots
of spilled tea fill the years
with such a weight
that it sags the porch

before the door, that's now
just a plywood plug?
It had to be more than winter
that dulled the yard
to seeping grey thistles and burrs.
Horses must once have stood waiting,
bending a hoof,
where saw-horses lean now,
on the toolbox and cord.
My ears redden in sliding-down day.
I turn from the house
and look up the track,
hoping to see the white light
round and growing
on the wide, warming train,
the white light throwing silver spears
in all directions.
When the train comes, I'll go.
But the old house will wait.
For the workers and the tools.
And when they come to it,
when they come to the house,
will they be working to bring it back?
Or working to bring it down?

Fall Leaves Fall

The fall leaves fall
into the summer shadows

of their trees; a maple shape
on the drowsy grass,

a willow by the creek,
the round, hiding dogwood.

Impatient morning
and the wind of my car

fail to chase these leaves
away. They riffle and rattle

and flutter. They settle again
like shadows beside the road,

to lie where trees
and the season finish them.

Something I Could Not Tell You

I wanted the hill more than home
and fevered guilt rose with my wanting.
I wanted the hill of dripping daisies and moss;
a soft stalk of hay to chew to green juice.
I wanted to climb the hill
and force the village far and down,
and laugh from that high green place;
no trace of grief or trembled remembering.
You wore out with work, ending your day and days
tired, shrunk, drunk, frowning, glowering, dead.
I wanted the hill and a twitchy hound,
a white-tipped tail, a pillow, a yip;
to only stalk butterflies and woodchuck holes.
I wanted the hill and a leaf-curled book
of maidens and forests and kings.
Kings who killed; kings who blessed
the page and broke the holy snow.
I wanted the hill more than home.

What Is Seen

The sun rolls high, harsh; burning
summer to brittle autumn.

Tall trees flare above small trees
to catch the light and break it.

They break it and juggle
the pieces. The small tree cowers

dimmed by the tall;
darkened in homage

to size, in a place
to hide and be lovely.

Someone Else's Supper

Go to the house
where you grew up.

Sit by the side of the road
outside what you cannot enter.

The black-trunk maples stoop to see
if you're someone they know.

When the pines lining
the fence have grown tall

and wild-haired
over the goldenrod

you wove into forts
and swords,

go to the house
where you grew up.

Learn that the poplars went
when the road widened;

the poplars who showed
to the wind the silver

sides of their leaves.
Find the roof new, slanted, strange.

Go to the house
where you grew up;

see the toss-and-catch scars
on the boy-blessed lawn healed.

Ball bats and sleds—
grayed, splintered, gone.

The light in the kitchen of the house
where you grew up

sits over someone else's supper.
And the other windows are dark

under the trees, beside green hedges
circling the house where you grew up.

Aftermath

Two days after the blizzard
I crunch on stucco snow,
packed on the roofs,
packed on the lawns,
pulling air down in blue
shadows. Oak limbs spread
against the china sky;
twigs poke from the drifts.
The winded ridges
and the rubble of the plows
burn day to more day
than winter allows;
a battle won in a lost war.
The already dead
cannot die more.
And the sun works twice:
in blinding white light;
and by laying shades
across March and me
of all that outlives winter
and all that will glow
when the snow is gone.

Age

He lies on his mussed bed
reading. Damn. As if
the smudged, scratched glasses,
weren't enough, his eyes reflect
in the lenses. Wrinkles
sluice across his lids
and cheeks, in the prescribed
mirror. They look like
the plowing around
elderly eyes.
Age snaps through him
smelling of acrid air
and defecting hair.
Age groans in his head
as he lies reading on his bed.
Elbow aches; dandruff flakes;
sneaky age snakes
through him
like browned grass
on the baseball field
limped to autumn, mitts away.
He feels dust seeping
into his soul.

Night

Inside the Kendall station
a flourescent light
edges with white
the dented, splintered work bench.
Through the square panes
of the rollered-down door locked tight,
I see wrenches
and bolts
and oily iron pieces
sitting in that light
as if they sit in prayer.

Outside the Kendall station
a mercury-vapor street lamp
has its work
interrupted by the leaves
of the still-night maples
and the hundred closing fingers
of the dark.
And all I hear
are crickets and frogs
making dew
in the air
for the morning.

There Comes Each Year One Fall Day

There comes each year one fall day
to which the sun is not invited.
The sky, a flat chalk cloud, pricks
the air with mist. And the weight
of that mist on the raging
leaves is the last life asks
them to handle. They yield
as the season demands and lie
upon the grass. And all the while
the wind, in the bird-forsaken trees,
all the while the wind drones
dust-to-dust in light too dark
to be day.

About the Author

Ira Joe Fisher holds an MFA from New England College and currently teaches poetry at the University of Connecticut at Stamford. His poetry has appeared in various literary journals and he is the author of the chapbook *Rememberng Rew*, now in its second printing. Fisher appears weekly on the *The Saturday Early Show* for CBS, and has worked in radio and television for over forty years. He and his wife, Shelly, and their four children live in Connecticut.

About the *NYQ Poetry Series*

The *NYQ Poetry Series* was established by Athanata Arts in cooperation with *The New York Quarterly* to present a series of book-length collections by poets published in the *The New York Quarterly*.

For more information visit *www.nyqpoetryseries.com*

Printed in the United States
60504LVS00002B/10-33